Buses in Colour - Volume Three

THE LEYLAND NAT

Paul Chancellor

2 CORNLANDS ROAD
via Acomb Road

363

LEYLAND
NATIONAL

PNW 603W

The **Buses In Colour** Series™

is produced under licence by

Nostalgia Road Publications Ltd.
Units 5-8, Chancel Place, Shap Road Industrial Estate,
Kendal, Cumbria, LA9 6NZ
Tel.+44 (0)1539 738832 - Fax: +44 (0)1539 730075

designed and published by
Trans-Pennine Publishing Ltd.
PO Box 10, Appleby-in-Westmorland, Cumbria, CA16 6FA
Tel.+44 (0)17683 51053 Fax.+44 (0)17683 53558
e-mail:admin@transpenninepublishing.co.uk

and printed by
Kent Valley Colour Printers Ltd.
Kendal, Cumbria +44(0)1539 741344

Front Cover: *John Fishwick & Sons Ltd. of Leyland, Lancashire were located very close to the famous vehicle manufacturers that carried the town's name. Therefore they were an enthusiastic operator of the firm's products, including No.34 (XCW 957R) which is seen at Southport on rally duty.*

Rear Cover Top: *Westlink became a semi-autonomous unit within the London Transport empire. Yet, despite its non-standard livery, LTR ownership can be established by the vehicles used, including some from the large batch of LT Mk1 Nationals.*

Rear Cover Bottom: *Crosville was one of the largest operators of the B-Series 10.3m Nationals, as exemplified by this line up at the Flint Depot.*

Title Page: *The City of York was a great place to visit if you wanted to watch Leyland Nationals at work. The City's services were a mix of urban and rural work, on which this type of bus performed ably. Initially operated by a division of the West Yorkshire Road Car Co. (York-West Yorks) the services and many of the vehicles later went on to Yorkshire Rider. Prior to transfer, WRCC 363 (PNW 603W), a Mk2 model, is seen heading east from the imposing railway station.*

This Page: *Northwich, a former North West Road Car depot, came into the Crosville empire under an NBC re-organisation and was soon inundated with Nationals. It was also the base for a small number painted in the blue and cream 'Mid-Cheshire' livery as seen here.*

THE LEYLAND NATIONAL - AN INTRODUCTION

This is a personal tribute to the Leyland National, which was born following the formation of the National Bus Company (NBC) in 1969. Although there were nominally several vehicle Marques available to the British bus operator, e.g. AEC, Bristol, Leyland, the market was almost entirely controlled by British Leyland, because it owned many of these companies; furthermore, the group also controlled part of the body building market via its ownership of Eastern Coach Works. Meanwhile, the NBC no doubt believed that as the single buyer of Leyland psv chassis, it ought to be specifying exactly what it required from a supplier.

Thus it undoubtedly made sense for the largest producer and the largest customer to work together; indeed with hindsight, we might even ask could they have actually lived without each other? So, enter the Leyland National as a joint venture between the two. This revolutionary integral vehicle was to be produced at a new factory in Cumbria and would replace the Bristol RE, the AEC Reliance and the Leyland Leopard for single-deck bus operation.

Above: *This is a far cry from the congestion of suburbia that surrounded these buses when they entered service with London Country. By 1985, NPD 144L and NDP 165L had migrated west to became South Wales Transport's numbers 831 and 833 respectively.*

The repercussions of this move were to be quite dramatic on the British bus industry. The National was quite a complex machine and thus it did not immediately appeal to independent operators who had traditionally bought new vehicles, whilst the numerous municipal operators were suddenly faced with a substantially reduced choice of vehicles! It was therefore almost a case of the Leopard or the National, unless the light-weight chassis such as Bedford or Ford were to be considered.

Yet, you can't fight progress and in the 1970s Nationals in their thousands rolled off the production line at Lillyhall, near Workington. The bottom line was that you could have a 10.3-metre or 11.3-metre bus (although there was a 10.9-metre option) and it could be either single or dual-door. The Leyland 510 power unit was standard, as was a forced air ventilation system.

3

Top Left: *As well as operating dual-door National buses in its 'city fleet', Bristol Omnibus allocated a small number of such vehicles to its Cheltenham operation. Here 1430 (JHU 871L) is seen at its home depot, wearing the standard NBC Leaf Green livery.*

Bottom Left: *The first Leyland National for Midland Red, and the only one to appear in pre-NBC livery, was Fleet No.101 (HHA 101L). In this view it is seen in its NBC guise, but it has since been returned to its former glory by First Group and can still be seen in Redditch on occasions, albeit mainly used for driver training.*

Although envisaged as a service bus, if an operator asked nicely (and paid more), dual-purpose examples could be provided in which coach seats were fitted. The resulting examples were not, however, passenger friendly and several complaints were received. Naturally, in common with any new design, there were lots of teething problems, no doubt exacerbated by the complexity of the machine. Yet, that familiar rattling engine noise and a smoky out-pouring from the fishtail exhaust pipe soon became familiar sounds and sights across the country.

More than 3,000 were produced in the Phase 1 build of the first style of National before major modifications were made. At first, the model codes took the following form, where (using as an example) 1151/1R/0402, the first four digits (1151) denoted the length and engine type (11.3-metre/510 engine), whilst the next couple (1R) stood for single door, right-hand-drive and the final four (0402) described everything from engine ratings to extra fan fittings. Subsequently the coding changed to just describe the length and engine e.g.: 11351 followed by 1R for single door, right hand drive (11351/1R). Design modifications were introduced from build number 3,331 onwards and these became known as Phase 2 models.

A big deterrent to purchasing these buses was their cost. Due to the deteriorating state of the market putting pressure on NBC, this problem was overcome by a cheap version known as the B series launched in 1979. The easy way to spot a B series model was the fact that the ventilation pod had gone, whilst heating was provided by the traditional underfloor heaters. Only 10.3-metre versions were offered in the B series. Hot on the heels of the B series came the Mk2 in 1980. The radiator conventionally moved to the front of the vehicle , and this re-location gave rise to the distinctive bulbous front. This move was to allow for the fitting of a larger engine, as the MkI models were infamous for their poor turn of speed, especially when fully loaded.

There was also the market imperative of trying to increase sales to non-NBC customers, mainly because demand within the NBC was falling, especially as the fleet replacement cycle was completed. Also looming just around the corner was the minibus revolution, privatisation and deregulation.

Under the new scheme, a Leyland 690 or L11 engine was offered. but so too were two Gardner products that were guaranteed to endear themselves to certain members of the industry. Certainly the National Mk2 found a wider range of customers than its predecessor before being replaced by the Leyland Lynx after just five years. The model designation also evolved with the Mk2 and there was a slight increase in length to 10.6- or 11.6-metres. If the roof-mounted heating system was fitted, an 'A' appeared in the code followed by the engine type e.g. 116AHLXB/IR.

The 1980s brought about rapid changes in the bus industry. Suddenly 'small' was great, both in terms of operating unit and vehicle sizes, as the NBC was broken up into little companies ready for privatisation. At the same time, licensing regulations were relaxed. Then, to try to stop others muscling in on their patches, vast numbers of mini-buses were deployed. This of course posed a problem, namely what to do with all of those relatively modern Nationals? The outcome was that there were frequent moves of vehicles between operators as the buses were cascaded around the country to match fleet age imbalances.

They were also brought in to counter short-term extra vehicle requirements to tackle competitive activities. However, the foibles of the earlier machines also led to many premature withdrawals. The NBC had developed a policy of never allowing their withdrawn vehicles to go on the second-hand market, but as the empire crumbled, so too did the policy and it wasn't long before independents across the land were running 'used' Nationals. In some cases the complexity didn't matter, as they were run until they broke, then they were used for spares as a replacement was acquired from a dealer.

But it was not all gloom and doom. Some former NBC operators decided that the body of a National was too good to throw away and various re-engineering plans were consequently put in place. In most cases, the first thing to go was the Leyland 510 engine! Overall their efforts must have succeeded because until relatively recently, examples were still to be seen in daily use across the country. It is only now, with the youngest machines approaching their 35th birthday, that the sight and sounds of the Leyland National are fading from our streets.

Below: *An ex-Northern General example is seen dumped at the Midland Red West Redditch depot in June 1985, but no fleet number is visible. Yet, the Northern practice of moving the number plate up onto the bodywork allows the vehicle to be identified as NCN 974L.*

POPPY RED

The main colours of the early Leyland National buses were either Poppy Red or Leaf Green, as the following pages show.

Above: *This was not a Ribble bus with a baggage trolley; it was, in fact an experimental electrically-powered National with a trailer of batteries in tow.*

Left: *Cumberland Motor Services, being the NBC unit on the doorstep of the manufacturing plant at Lillyhall, received some of the first units off the production line. Being one of the smaller NBC units, Cumberland never had a vast fleet, but this view of 361 (NAO 361M) taken at Workington, shows the early 'long' roof-mounted pod.*

Right: *Thousands of the vehicles that flowed from Lillyhall were painted in these colours, which Derek Stead (a spray painter at the plant) recalled that "it tended to get a bit monotonous." The NBC was always looking for economies and omitting white bands (such as those seen on Cumberland 361) from vehicles saved a few pounds here and there. Take PUK 633R of Midland Red West as it displays 'all-over' red at Redditch bus station. The National did not look too bad in this livery but vehicles with larger bodywork panels, especially double-deckers, did not suit un-relieved red or green.*

Below: *The subject of this 1974 view, is East Kent's EFN 178L in un-relieved Poppy Red not long after delivery. It is surrounded by vehicles of an earlier era, and they provide an interesting contrast with the then new NBC corporate colours.*

GREEN CREDENTIALS

Today, being 'green' means low-pollution vehicles, and the Leyland National (with its smoky emissions) could never have laid claim to such worthwhile credentials. However, next to Poppy Red, the next prominent colour to be found in the Leyland National production statistics, was Leaf Green. So we will now look at a few examples in that scheme.

Top Left: *Given the fleet size, Western and Southern National had relatively few National models, their routes being suited to the lighter and shorter Bristol LH. Here, a Southern National example is 2869 (AFJ 708T) photographed in the summer of 1986.*

Middle Left: *The idea in the standard NBC colours, was that they at least gave some hint to the original livery of the operator. In the new corporate colours, United Counties employed around a hundred-strong fleet of Leyland Nationals, typified by an immaculate 555 (ERP 555T) leaving Bedford Depot in March 1986.*

Bottom Left: *A typical NBC National of the 11351A/1R variety was Provincial 68 (SPR 40R).*

Bottom Right: *Overall, few external modifications took place to the NBC fleet of Nationals. Thus any livery variations accounted for much of the enthusiast interest at the time. Here LNI 3069 (TTC 535T) of Bristol Omnibus carries a Bath local identity as well as the later 'Badgerline' branding in September 1985.*

Above: *Despite some Leyland Nationals being 'green buses, they left a significant tell-tale in a cloud of blue smoke that emanated from the rear as we can see in this view. Here an ex-London Country example (NPD 138L), by then with Hastings & District, has returned to the capital on a National Express 037 Service duplicate on a weekend when there was a national rail strike.*

Bottom Right: *Here, CBV 778S has exchanged Poppy Red paint for green. New to Ribble, it then moved south to work for Southdown but retained the same fleet number, 778, as seen in this 1990 view adjacent to Portsmouth railway station. Despite the fact the Leyland Nationals were not exactly environmentally-friendly, this bus does carry an advert, publicising the local 'Green Card' travel scheme.*

MIXED SHADES

Above: *As times progressed, some fleets had examples of both red and green machines. Here we have all angles on the Leyland National series at Stroud bus station in March 1985; front, side, rear, with and without pod, even a B series 10.3-metre version and some REs to compare them with.*

Bottom Left: *Devon General was a separate entity under BET, but when the NBC was formed it came under Western National. However it was allowed to maintain its individuality, accentuated by the use of Poppy Red for its livery rather than Leaf Green. However, the two met at Torquay, where Mk1s VOD 604, VOD 625S and PTT 89R were pictured on a chilly December day in 1987.*

CHANGING NAMES

From time to time NBC indulged in the practice of moving vehicles between fleets. On other occasions, cast offs from one fleet just happened to meet a short fall at another.

Top Right: *Still at work in May 1985, Northern General twins BPT 907-8S fleet numbers 4627 and 4628 are seen peeping out at Chester-le-Street depot - a location my editor passed every day on his way to work in Newcastle in the late 1970s.*

Below: *A year later, whilst some of its fellows had gone for scrap, Northern NCN 951L had found a new home just down the road with United Automobile, where it became fleet number 3694. It is seen in Middlesbrough in 1986.*

DUAL PURPOSES

As stated in the introduction, the National could be ordered in dual-purpose specification, although the number of such vehicles accounted for only a small percentage of the total build.

Above: *Maidstone & District had a batch of ten dual-purpose Leyland Nationals, of which 3902 (SKN 902R) was the second in the batch. They could often be seen working into the heart of the capital.*

Bottom Left: *Crosville appeared to love the Leyland National and operated one of the largest fleets in the NBC empire. This included a large number of dual-purpose examples as typified by ENL 923 (HFM 179N).*

Top Right: *The dual-purpose versions received a different livery to standard service buses in the Corporate NBC scheme. This adopted the red or green colour scheme on the panels below the waist-line, with the National White coaching livery above. However, there were many variations on a theme! For instance, whilst Cheltenham & Gloucester vehicle LNI 3041, purports to be a dual-purpose vehicle, closer inspection of the photographs will reveal that only some seats are of the coach-type; those used on the raised section at the rear are standard bus seats.*

Middle Right: *Looking like a dual-purpose bus, UHG 754R was in fact a standard Ribble service bus, which became fleet number 654 in the Midland Red West sequence. It was pictured whilst working the Birmingham-Redditch service via Bromsgrove in June 1988.*

Bottom Right: *This was always intended to be a dual-purpose vehicle, as shown by its code number ND4175; this stood for 'National, dual-purpose, 41st vehicle of the 1975 delivery programme'. It was also a full-length vehicle, short versions being coded NS. At least the reference books were not needed to work out the vehicle details for National Welsh KDW 349P at Aberdare.*

Bottom Left: *Because of the rural nature of many of its routes, a feature of the National Welsh fleet was its use of the dual-purpose version of the National. which in due course qualified for the NBC stripe treatment as displayed by NWO 467R in 1989.*

BEING DIFFERENT

It would not be correct to say that only the three colours of Poppy Red, Leaf Green and National White were used at Lillyhall's paint shops, as the boredom was often relieved by the application of a different hue. The Tyne & Wear PTE 'Yellow' used on the Northern General National buses is a good example, whilst blue buses were also occasionally produced.

Top & Middle Left: *One of Northern's early models, 4408 (originally 27K, UUP 827K), poses at Stanley, Co. Durham. A later arrival, OCN 743M, is devoid of the white waist-band stripe, and has Northern decals on the front rather than the NBC twin-arrow logo.*

Bottom Left: *When Northern began to down-size its National fleet, Crosville clearly couldn't get enough of a good thing and they purchased Northern NCN 960L; although this was possibly only used for spares. Note the circular panel underneath the right screen, which allowed buses to be connected up to a hot air system to pre-heat the inside prior to going out on cold days.*

Bottom Right: *A hybrid livery if ever there was one. New to Crosville, EMB 642S was (in the course of their livery developments) given this green and white scheme. The management then decided that a small part of the Crosville empire should pass to Midland Red North and a new livery was applied. So here we have the temporary result of that decision, with 1042 as a white and green Midland Red bus at Oswestry in March 1992.*

Above: *No fewer than three of the small Jones fleet of Leyland Nationals are on show in this wintry view in 1981. I believe that Jones was the only fleet to initially operate blue Nationals; East Yorkshire Motor Services were the only other constituent to be tempted by NBC Blue, and they avoided Nationals like the plague for many years, and by the time they did take some into their ownership, the fleet had been painted in Poppy Red.*

Bottom Right: *Even by January 1985, blue-painted examples of the Leyland National in NBC fleets were somewhat of a rarity, but this was added to the City of Gloucester fleet as the NBC corporate image faded ahead of the big sell off. This bus, JHU 874L started life as a dual-door machine before being converted to a single-entrance layout and re-numbered accordingly.*

COATS OF MANY COLOURS

As the pre-privatisation changes to the NBC began to take affect, a series of brighter, more colourful liveries began to appear to replace Poppy Red and Leaf Green.

Top Left: *Although it sports a new livery, there can be little doubt about the operating company of this 10.3-metre National. However, Lincolnshire Road Car added to its indigenous fleet of Nationals with various purchases including this ex-London Country example, HPF 323N.*

Top Right: *On the split up of Alder Valley, City of Oxford acquired some operations in High Wycombe. In the inherited fleet came a number of Leyland Nationals and here 1356 (NPJ 481R) is seen at work in the town under its new ownership during 1995.*

Middle Left: *Although showing Eastern Counties decals, this view dates to after operations in Cambridgeshire had been hived off. Eastern Counties had a considerable number of Nationals, whilst the slimmed down firm even bought some ex-LT examples for driver training work. However, as PVF 353R seen in this 1988 view was an Eastern Counties original.*

Bottom Left: *Wearing a pseudo British Rail Inter-City livery, National No277 (TPE 170S) was run by Alder Valley North on a disabled-accessible service from Heathrow Airport to connect with various London main line terminal stations 20-years ago.*

Top Right: *Here we have a fairly basic variation on the Leaf Green and National White waist-band on Bristol Omnibus LN1 3025 (KHT 123P). This was an 11.3-metre model, which in its single door form was not hugely popular with Bristol. The company had placed some 340 Bristol REs in service by the time the National came along, but it had a greater need for short buses. Whilst this need was met by purchasing over 100 Bristol LHs, they also put into service some batches of both the 10.3-metre pod and B versions of the Mk1 National. By the time this 1986 view, the ownership of the company had gone on to Badgerline.*

Middle Right: *East Midland Motor Services had not operated vast numbers of Nationals as an NBC fleet, but a little topping up of the stock came in the shape of 508 (TWN 749N). This was an 11.3-metre LN1, which had formerly been with South Wales Transport, but by October 1989 it was to be seen much further north and entering Mansfield bus station.*

Bottom Right: *One of the earlier acquisitions by Stagecoach was the former NBC operation of East Kent. Little time was lost in applying the new owner's standard livery. However, as can be seen in this view of MFN 115R, the effect was lost as soon as a full side advert was applied to the vehicle.*

Bottom Left: *Trent were quite an enthusiastic operator of Mk1 Nationals although they did carry out some quite extensive modifications to their vehicles. Here, Trent's number 429 (KVO 429P) was captured on film whilst working on a local service in Nottingham in 1993.*

Above: *Complementing the standard NBC Leaf Green colour scheme, and looking a little better than the normal white band, was this pale green stripe employed by London Country North. For many enthusiasts, this was harking back to the original Green Line livery. In this particular view, this 'pod-less Mk1, fleet number SNB 484, is actually a 10351/B model, seen at work in Watford in 1990. Another identifying feature of these types was the nine louvres in the front panel.*

Bottom Left: *Although bland colour schemes could still be found on many Leyland National buses during the 1980s, interesting paint schemes did start to appear. Here we see a clever combination of advertising and route marketing, when this LN1 was seen at Gloucester Bus Station in September 1985. It is rather unfortunate that the bus is not actually working on the service that it is promoting. Rather, 3059 (TAE 641S) was pictured on the 419 route to Cheltenham.*

18

Top Left: *What appears to be United 3079 (EPT 879S) poses in this 1992 view, but all is not quite what it seems! The location is Trent's Langley Mill depot, after 3079 had been acquired by the midlands operator.*

Top Right: *By way of contrast, this very smart looking Mk1, 3090 (JBR 690T) is still in the United fleet. It is seen standing at Middlesbrough Bus Station in June 1986 before setting off on the nearly two hour-long 255 route to Whitby.*

Middle Right: *The movement of National buses from one operation to another was quite common in the 1980s, with some exciting new liveries appearing as a consequence. For example, Stevenage services were part of the London Country empire until the break up of the group. They were thereafter operated by Luton & District, itself a spin off from United Counties. In this de-centralisation strategy, Luton & District assumed control of certain services and adopted the Stevenage Bus local identity for this former London Country National, YPF 769T. Careful examination of the seats, which are visible through the windows, will reveal that this is not a dual-purpose vehicle, although some passengers might have thought it to be so on first observation.*

Bottom Right: *Another operation, Harrow Buses, was spun off from the main London Transport fleet and it took some Leyland Nationals with it. Seen in Watford in 1990, THX 234S was typical of more than 400 Mk1 models to ply their trade on the streets of the capital. This individual has escaped the confines of the city however to serve suburbia.*

SEEING RED

Several operators saw major changes to their fleet of Leyland National buses, but with Midland Red being my local operator, I was able to keep track of the changes within this company as an example of the period.

Above: *All was not well with Midland Red 489 (JOX 489P) as it would appear that the tow hook has had to be used to bring it back into Redditch depot. The minimalistic paint scheme looks particularly 'tatty' in this view.*

Bottom Left: *Another, less than pristine Midland Red West vehicle acquired the fleet number 170 on arrival from Northern General to partially match the registration NCN 970L.*

Top Right: *One of the earlier 'long pod' Nationals in the Midland Red fleet was 254 NHA 254M. By the time of this particular view in 1984, it had passed to Midland Red West fleet, and carries the Severnlink branding when seen at the former Angel Place Bus Station in Worcester.*

Middle Right: *Another Midland Red West National, this time 542 (NOE 542R) can be seen as it approaches the Angel Place terminus in Worcester overtaking a local independent's Willowbrook-bodied vehicle in the process.*

Bottom Right: *In this view another Midland Red West National in the 'modified Poppy Red' livery, 276 (NHA 276M), takes on the familiar 'lean-to' position as it rolls out of the re-built Redditch bus station in March 1986 as it works the 221 service Alcester.*

Bottom Left: *Here we have a picture that shows when a Midland Red livery wasn't red, for the vehicle has assumed Highway Safety Yellow to reflect a brand new role within the organisation. Midland Red were another fleet with a very large number of Leyland National models in service, one of which was 101 (HHA 101L). This vehicle, as will be recalled from page 4 of this book, was the first Leyland National for Midland Red and the only one to appear in a pre-NBC livery with the fleet. After many years in passenger service, it was transferred to the Driver Training fleet where it acquired the all-over yellow paint scheme. Who could have predicted back in the 1970s, that 101 would still been in use as the company's driver trainer unit at the start of 2007?*

21

Top Left: *Of the four Midland Red constituents, South perhaps tried the hardest to hark back to pre-NBC days with its rendition of the fleet name and livery. When this picture was taken on 12th October 1991, 586 (NOE 586R) was working on service in Coventry.*

Middle Left: *In contrast to the above, Midland Red West's Mk1 National 607, doesn't quite catch the spirit of the former Midland Red operation. In March 1986, NOE 607R heads away from Redditch Bus Station on the Lodge Park circular service.*

Bottom Left: *Moves around the network didn't help either, but they did provide some interesting sightings. Red Nationals were not that common in Cornwall but former Midland Red GOL 423N found itself sent on a 'busman's holiday' at Camborne depot in early-1984. At the age of just eight-years, it was probably ousted from its former home territory by the vast influx of minibuses that had started to penetrate the various Midland Red operations and services.*

Bottom Right: *Midland Red had approaching 600 Nationals on its books by the time production of the Mk2 eventually ceased, and in anybody's terms, this was a significant vote of confidence in the model. As stated, the Nationals were systematically replaced from the fleet by smaller vehicles during the 1980s. Here, in a picture from June 1986, we have 426 (GOL 426N) that was allocated to Midland Red South at Leamington. Note the contrasting colour changes on the four front bumpers seen on this page.*

Above: *This view, taken at Redditch in 1984, illustrates the time of change just engulfing the industry as GOL 420N carries Midland Red fleet names whilst the National behind has had Midland Red West branding applied to the white band above the windows.*

Bottom Right: *Worcester local services all seemed to be in the hands of Leyland Nationals such as 474 (JOX 474P) seen here. As part of the privatisation plan, these were replaced by more than 60 Mercedes mini-buses. The following replacement cycle saw larger Mercedes mini-buses take over but their reign was short lived. The wheel has almost gone full circle with several Worcester services currently being worked by Wright-bodied Dennis Lance models cast off from London, in some cases complete with dual door bodies.*

Above: *Following the split of Midland Red into four parts, each new company applied its own distinctive livery. In this view, JOX 472P, displays the Midland West Red Wyvern logo to good effect at Redditch in February 1991. The Wyvern has long been associated with the Midlands, particularly on the crest of the old Midland Railway during the Victorian and Edwardian era. However its origins go back much further as the mythical beast, similar to a dragon, and it was once well used in heraldry and was even the emblem of the Kings of Wessex.*

Bottom Left: *Several of the new operations within the new operation maintained a 'red' theme to their colour schemes, although some were quite radical. Coming up to its 'sell by' date, Midland Red West 270 (NHA 270M) is seen on service 319 in Bromsgrove in 1990.*

Top Left: *At the time of writing, Midland Red is celebrating its centenary, and it commemorated the event with National 101 (HHA 101L), which has reverted back to a 'red' livery. However, what followed the NBC red schemes at Midland Red West might be described as pleasant, but not inspiring (as seen on 533 JOX 533P). This of course contrasts with the red-liveried West buses that had the white band between the windows and the roof panels seen elsewhere in this book.*

Top Right: *Midland Red North applied this scheme to its vehicles and used the name Mercian, again to create something of a local feel. As with most things white, it looked very smart at the outset but after a few months or so at work in the Midlands it could look a little less than appealing. Seen hard at work in 1998, JOX 530P is still active some 20-years after delivery.*

Middle Right: *Can't you just tell that this green National is a Midland Fox? Well not at first sight, but the fleet number 3641 gives away the identity of PUK 641R as it runs through a box junction in Leicester city centre in 1990, with a Barton coach seen to the right.*

Bottom Right: *The firm had a large fleet of dual purpose vehicles (Leyland Leopard coach chassis with both Plaxton and Marshall bodywork), but they nevertheless decided that they still did not have sufficient express vehicles and tried to transform some standard Leyland Nationals with a nice coat of paint. A small batch of JOX/Ps in the Midland Red West fleet based at Redditch were given the 'Midland Express' livery treatment, of which 485 (JOX 485P) was one example.*

In The Marches and The Valleys

The use of Nationals outside England was initially not very large, but as the years passed, quite big fleets became established, especially in Wales.

Above: *Welsh Nationalism is seen at Red & White's Cwmbran depot in May 1992. Third in line is a former Bristol HEU 121N, whilst the other red bus appears to be ex-Midland Red.*

Bottom Left: *The Cheltenham & District fleet had long been part of the Bristol Omnibus empire, but it had retained its distinctive red livery, although the red liveried vehicles had not strayed far from the town. After the changes in the fleet 3022, KHT 120P is seen at Stroud.*

Top Right: *A smart livery in good condition could really set off the lines on the Leyland National and this version of the later Red & White livery seen at Chepstow in May 1992 does just that.*

Middle Right: *However, when a paint job was coming to the end of its working-life, the story was quite the opposite. For instance, looking a bit worse for wear National Welsh N609 (SKG 741R) stands at Newport on a gloomy day in March 1990. The original NBC National Welsh fleet bought Leyland Nationals in considerable numbers, as they appeared to have little use for double-deckers. However, the company's purchases only ever covered the Mk1 type, and the later versions that joined the fleet were never obtained as new vehicles.*

Bottom Right: *Here we have a view of one of South Wales Transport's original Nationals, as opposed to one of those that it acquired second-hand. This bus, fleet number 773 (JTH 773P), acquired this multi-coloured 'deck-chair' livery along with the rest of the fleet upon de-regulation and was seen in Swansea waiting to work route 11 to Mayhill in 1986.*

Bottom Left: *Next we see a local identity on a traditional NBC background, with National Welsh NS1456 (KKL 527P) as it stands next to another member in the fleet (NS1559). It can be seen proudly displaying the New Rhondda vinyls on its traditional Poppy Red livery, however this was not a Welsh National vehicle from new, but one transferred into the area from far-away Maidstone & District.*

LOCAL APPLICATIONS

The National was not a vehicle that appealed to municipal undertakings, due to its high purchase costs, but the PTEs liked them, and as small local 'units' were formed as part of the NBC sell-off, it became a very different story.

Above: *Halton Transport was an exception to the poor municipal up-take of the National, for at one time nearly all of this fleet was made up of this type. With the Runcorn-Widnes bridge stands No. 7 (LMB 947P), in the red and cream livery.*

Bottom Left: *Tyne & Wear PTE had a small fleet of Nationals, of which KBB 522L later found employment with Burnley & Pendle and is seen at Burnley in 1985.*

Top Right: *Several National buses ended up seeing service with the larger Passenger Transport Executive fleets, and we have shown a Tyneside example on the previous page. Here we see a Greater Manchester PTE example working on home territory, with No.157 (JVM 981N) getting ready to depart with the 328 service from Stockport Bus Station in 1984.*

Below: *No fewer than 11 of Merseyside PTE's Nationals are to be seen in this view taken in 1985. Both the Mk1 and Mk2 models were operated and there were even a small number of coach-seated examples in the Merseyside fleet. The PTE was formed in 1969 from the fleets of Birkenhead, Liverpool and Wallasey and in 1974 the PTE was then joined by the municipal fleets of St. Helens and Southport. Post de-regulation, the bus operation traded for a while as Merseybus before becoming Merseyside Transport Holdings Ltd.*

Top Left: *Formerly working for London Country as SNB223, LBP 223P had moved to Welwyn and Hatfield upon privatisation and was photographed in the Welwyn Hatfield Line livery, whilst heading for the bus station on 19th April 1991. The use of local names was coming back into vogue in the early-1990s, as passenger-loyalty seemed very much orientated to this concept.*

Middle Left: *When they were new to the West Midlands PTE, the extensive fleet of Leyland Nationals bore the Executive's traditional blue and cream colours. However, it seems as though the PTE were to become trendsetters when they replaced the traditional cream colour with silver! The choice of this colour was also ahead of its time, as nearly every other car on the roads these days seems to be finished in silver. This particular example bears a Wolverhampton fleet name, quite a short lived adornment, and a Wolverhampton destination blind; so there are no prizes for guessing the location of this photograph of 1806 (OOX 806R), which was taken on 20th July 1996.*

Bottom Left: *A good load is carried by Hartlepool's smart-looking 11.3-metre Mk1 Leyland National. It carries fleet number 15, but it also bears the Darlington registration mark SHN 415R. The Mk1 Nationals did not really find favour in this municipal fleet, as all their efforts looked to be being made to keep its predecessor, their fleet of Bristol REs on the road instead.*

Top Right: *For a brief period, West Midlands Passenger Transport Executive held the contract for the tendered service from Stourbridge to Redditch and on this route it employed a few of their large number of Leyland Nationals. Here, fleet number 1852 (TVP 852S), is captured on film as it lays over at Redditch Bus Station.*

Bottom Right: *West Midlands PTE also employed a number of coach-seated 'dual-purpose' Nationals in its fleet. As these were basically 'coaching' standard vehicles, they regularly worked excursions to 'far-flung places' at different times. In the case pictured here, it was Cheltenham for the Gold Cup Meeting, where TVP 864S displays the 'reversed' blue and cream livery that the Passenger Transport Executive employed on the coaching fleet. The gold-coloured lettering adds to the more refined look of the National, which by any stretch of the imagination was never intended as a luxury coach.*

31

Top Left: *Continuing the theme of using 'local' bus company names, here we see Tees-liveried XGR 727R. This Mk1 model had been a Teesside resident for most of its operating life, having started out with United Automobile Services before passing to the Tees subsidiary at the time of the company fragmentation. It is pictured in the low autumnal sunlight found at Middlesbrough in 1991.*

Middle Left: *Local-authority control is also evident on RKA 869T, which is seen in Leeds on 26th June 1995. This was one of a very few Nationals that managed to move from one PTE organisation to another; it started life with Merseyside and then moved to Yorkshire Rider, of which Quickstep was a subsidiary company.*

Bottom Left: *Merthyr Tydfil Transport owned a number of Nationals that were painted in its traditional livery, even though WWO 637T is looking a little the worse for wear in this 1989 view. Merthyr was one of a small number of the municipal operators who simply had to shut up shop in the face of competition following Mrs. Thatcher's de-regulation of bus services.*

Bottom Right: *It's a far cry from the leafy lanes of Devon and Cornwall, the former home of VOD 602S, to the centre of Sheffield. Even so, as part of the Yorkshire Terrier fleet, this example saw out its final days working in the 'Steel City'. It is interesting to note that a Volvo badge has been fitted at the front of the bus, which suggests that an engine upgrade has taken place.*

INDEPENDENT SPIRITS

Towards the end of the NBC period many of the 'surplus' Nationals went to independent operators who acquired good vehicles at a relatively modest cost.

Above: *An early Mk1, PTF 730L was delivered new to Ribble, however when seen in 1993 it had become Birmingham Coach Company number 83.*

Bottom Right: *Brewers, was a separate 'independent' unit formed under the South Wales Transport umbrella. Thus SWT National JTH7 55P donned Brewers livery and gained a 'B' in front of its fleet number, when observed in Swansea on 19th October 1990.*

Top Left: *Here we have an independent National in action, in a livery marketed as Redline. This was a former Poppy Red vehicle that entered service as MCN 842L with the Northern General fleet. Since its move southwards, it has adopted a nice shade of blue topped off with some pinky-purple to serve the good folks of Milton Keynes. It is seen working the Bletchley service in November 1987.*

Middle Left: *Doncaster bus station is the setting for this view of former Bristol Omnibus JHU 870L, which found further gainful employment with the well known independent Wilfreda Beehive. The picture was taken in May 1992.*

Bottom Left: *For many years Peoples Provincial had minded its own business, running services around Gosport and Fareham in Hampshire. However, it spread its wings into Portsmouth following deregulation and acquired several Leyland Nationals, buying them from all and sundry to provide the extra vehicles needed to support this move. One such was an early Mk1 machine NPD 128L, which was formerly with London Country. It is seen in action in Portsmouth in 1990.*

Bottom Right: *Gainsborough was the location for VUA 152R in Barnards' fleet when seen in 1991. This MkI had operated as number 32 in the Yorkshire Woollen District fleet around Dewsbury in a previous life. The change from the hilly territory around the Spen Valley area to the relatively flat Lincolnshire countryside would probably be evident when following this bus up hill, as they were previously noted for their blue smoke when climbing the hills of West Yorkshire.*

Top Left: *Following privatisation, Sovereign operated a number of services in Hertfordshire. It was part of the Blazefield group (as were a number of companies in Yorkshire), which probably accounts for the arrival in the south of a B-type Series 1 National. Formerly DNW 843T was in the West Yorkshire Road Car fleet, but it was recorded in Stevenage by October 1995.*

Top Right: *One of the less common National types was the 10351A/1R (the 10.3-metre version) with full air circulation/heating. This one, DDW 430V operated in the Cynon Valley fleet as their number 30. I seem to remember that this fleet was called Aberdare UDC before Cynon Valley!*

Middle Right: *Further competition is seen in Portsmouth, with a Provincial National being pursued by its rivals. Provincial built up a considerable fleet of secondhand Nationals, which included a few ex-London Transport examples, including YYE 276T seen here on April Fool's Day 1995.*

Bottom Right: *Fishwicks of Leyland (who at the time of writing this book in 2007 are about to celebrate their centenary), had always been a staunch supporter of the local product. Indeed the fleet had contained many of the prototypes developed by Leyland. Despite the National being produced in Cumbria, the allegiance to Leyland remained and several Nationals joined the Fishwick fleet, which was quite a rarity in as much as few independent operators took them on from new. Here we see their 21 (HCW 762N) at the Leyland depot bearing the two-tone green livery with gold lettering.*

Top Left: *Classic of Anfield Plain, really went to town on this National, which they embellished with chrome wheel trims to set off their immaculate livery. This vehicle has been a bit of a mystery to me, and I have not been able to find any detail of its history prior to its arrival with Classic, and an enquiry to the company failed to reveal any detail either. It carries the registration KLL 844N, but this was not issued when new. A suggestion has been made that it might have been one of the un-registered Nationals that were originally used at Heathrow Airport.*

Top Right: *At the time of writing, Chase Bus Services were still using a large fleet of Nationals, many like BYW 418V coming from London Transport, which is seen on service in Walsall. Note the window at the rear, which has been modified for an air intake, no doubt required following the fitting of an alternative power unit. How long this firm would have continued to use the Nationals is now a matter of speculation, for following a take-over by Arriva an auction of such vehicles was announced in April 2007.*

Middle Left: *The livery and registration are a bit of a give-away as to the source of this vehicle, namely Midland Red West. However, by July 1997, it had moved north to Barnsley, where it is seen in service with an un-identified independent operator.*

Bottom Left: *No longer wearing the green of Crosville, this Mk2 National was part of the fleet of G. R. Kinch when seen in Nottingham in 1992.*

Top Right: *Things are not always what they seem as we can tell from this picture! Here we have a Wakefield City Bus running to Doncaster on the West Yorkshire Metro 211 service. This route was Barnsley Interchange, Cudworth, Grimethorpe, Brierley, South Elmsall and Doncaster Interchange; a total journey time of 80 minutes. The bus working this route in July 1997 is a 10.3-metre B series model, formerly with Crosville Motor Services.*

Middle Right: *An attempt at local service promotion in Bristol found this dual-door National (HHY 814N) from the Bristol City fleet working in this yellow and red scheme marketed under the City B Line banner.*

Bottom Right: *The origins of the Ambassador Travel, who were operating this particular Leyland National on 3rd July 1993 are lost in the mists of time; but it is not the operator of that name who were based in East Anglia. Neither do I think that there was any connection with London, despite the LT roundel on the side panels of the bus. Given the former Bristol ownership of JEU 571N and the location, which was the M5 near Weston-super-Mare, it may well be a firm based in the South West of England.*

Bottom Left: *A number of Nationals that used to belong to Greater Manchester PTE later found employment with independent operators. One such was HJA 125N, which is very smartly turned out when seen in Newcastle in 1987. A smart green and cream livery is here emblazoned with 'North Eastern' fleet names.*

37

Top Left: *In March 1997, a Mk1 long pod National (ORP 466M) runs into Bromsgrove on the service from Merry Hill shopping centre, when it was being operated by Ludlows, the Halesowen-based independent. This particular example had come from the United Counties and was one of a small number of Leyland National models in the Ludlows fleet.*

Below: *Red Bus was the name adopted by the Western/ Southern National subsidiary that was set up to take over services in North Devon. Registered HTA 844N, this was one of a small number of Nationals that were transferred with this operation. It was seen in Ilfracombe in September 1995, whilst it was on a service to Westward Ho, which is perhaps best known for being named after the novel of the same name written by Charles Kingsley.*

Above: *The 'new' Wilts & Dorset knew how to make vehicles last and carried out extensive refurbishment programmes to certain types in its fleet, including the Mk1 Nationals. Here we see a very smart example of a refurbished bus, as 3648 (GLJ 676N) works a service in Poole. It is 13th September 1990 and this vehicle has a few years left in it yet, nominally still being with its original operator by descendency.*

Bottom Right: *Redditch was the first town in the country to receive one of the new NBC local identity paint schemes. Reddibus was chosen and applied in the style seen here on 609. Next to it, 550, carried the more usual style of local branding on the roof band. However, the actual identity carried cannot be made out in this particular view.*

Top Left: *Alder Valley was a name conjured up by NBC when it amalgamated Thames Valley with Aldershot and District. The new enterprise operated a considerable number of Leyland Nationals including several MkI dual-purpose machines. Here however we see 200 HPJ 502N, one of the standard bus-seated vehicles, displaying the distinctive livery adopted by this fleet.*

Middle Left: *Having created Alder Valley at the start of the NBC era out of Thames Valley and Aldershot & District, the two parts were almost re-created to enable the privatisation to take place. The old Thames Valley territory was reincarnated as The Berks & Bucks Bus Company better known as Beeline and received its fair share of Mk1s into the bargain, of which GPJ 896N was one example.*

Bottom Left: *When Western National was split into four parts for the purposes of privatisation, its fleet of 100 Leyland Nationals did not give the constituent companies a large fleet of this type. One that was based in the Plymouth/East Cornwall part of the operation was PTT 82R, which carried the striking Cornwall Busways livery although retaining Western National legal lettering when pictured in February 1987.*

Bottom Right: *Northumbria was carved out of United Automobile Services to run routes north of the Tyne. A number of Nationals were transferred from the United fleet, but GPD 296N was a 10.3-metre coach-seated example from the London Country fleet. The normal Northumbria livery was red, white and blue, but the all-over white seen here in December 1989 might suggest either a hurried entry into service or a bus that was planned for early withdrawal.*

Top Left: *In the south, in NBC days Hants & Dorset had control of the Bournemouth and Southampton conurbations, whilst Wilts & Dorset looked after the routes emanating from Salisbury. The rearrangement of territories over the years has seen Hampshire Bus, which started life controlling all of the area to the east of Bournemouth, working out of Basingstoke, and Wilts & Dorset having control of Bournemouth and Poole. In 1985, Hampshire bus were running from Southampton using the ex-H&D National VFX 985S.*

Top Right: *Northwich depot went through an identity crisis under NBC. Formerly a North Western Road Car depot, it was then merged into Crosville. However, when it came to the big sell off, North Western was reborn along with a striking new livery replacing the slightly staid cream with stripes seen on the adjacent National. Seen in July 1990, CFM 351S and KMA 396T, are both 11.3-metre Mk1 machines.*

Middle Right: *Eastern National had a very large number of Leyland Nationals and when the fleet was split as part of the sell-off., Thamesway (one of the new operating companies) naturally gained a number of Nationals, 1879 (BNO 669T) being one of these.*

Bottom Right: *When Eastern Counties was split up for privatisation, like many of the other large NBC fleets, small units were formed. The vehicles operating around Cambridge formed Cambus, and they logically took Cambridge blue as the basis for their livery. Here, PVF 354R displays this livery as it awaits departure from Peterborough en-route to Cambridge.*

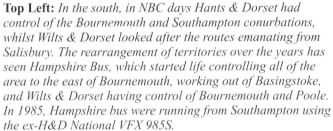

Left: *Stroud Valley's 3048 (SAE 751S) is seen on rally duty in August 1992. Despite its stylish new make-over, it still retained its former Bristol Omnibus number in the segregated fleet. It has to be said, even by the most traditional enthusiasts, that many of the 1980s and '90s liveries were a great improvement on the unrelieved green and red paint jobs of the 1970s.*

Below: *Once upon a time there was a small NBC unit called Brighton, Hove & District, then Southdown came along and took control, and the BH&D name all but disappeared. But like so many other companies, it re-emerged at the time of the NBC split and this time it took control of the former Southdown routes and vehicles in the Brighton and Hove areas. Thus PUF 40R had been Southdown 40 before swapping NBC Leaf Green for red and cream as captured in this 1991 shot.*

NEW IDEAS

The Mk2 National, built around the TL11 engine is an interesting story, and somewhat in-depth for this photographic album. Readers are therefore recommended to obtain an article by Ron Phillips that appeared in the Leyland Society's magazine *Leyland Torque* No.16, in the Summer of 2002.

Above: *A Scottish Mk2 is Midland Bluebird 49 (RFS 588V) seen at Falkirk in 1994. Many of these machines came south of the border long before their normal life expectancy of 15-years. Indeed they were survived by many much older Leopards with Alexander bodies in the Scottish Bus Group fleets.*

Bottom Right: *From the same batch, Midland Bluebird 41 (RFS 580V) waits for customers at Falkirk in 1994.*

Above: *Due to changing times and the politics in public transport, the Mk2 was not the success that the earlier model had been, and in many fleets they became everyday workhorses, soon assuming a 'tatty' condition. Southdown, however, always had a reputation for turning out immaculate vehicles. They started early with Nationals with a quantity of 'L-registered' examples and then took batches throughout the production run. This Mk2, fleet number 123 (HFG 923V), shows off its post-NBC livery in Portsmouth in 1992.*

Bottom Left: *This bevy of Mk2s, fleet numbers 133-4/6 (RUF 433-4/6X), represent roughly 10% of the total Southdown stock of this type in April 1987. Despite this Southdown's love of standardisation, each of these vehicles is in a slightly different version of the corporate livery.*

Top Right: *The Mk2 Nationals in Poppy Red and Leaf Green do not feature large in my photographic collection, as there always seemed something more colourful to photograph, but before we realised it they were all gone. Here we have one example of a service-livered Mk2, remarkably doing a duty you would not expect to find it on. Obviously, this is not your normal kind of National Express vehicle, but a bus-seated Mk2, No.119 of Southdown, which has been pressed into service for a 'Limited Stop' working. It is seen here passing London's Victoria railway station in August 1984, before returning to the nearby coach station in readiness for the homeward run. Registered GYJ 919V, the unrelieved green livery is thankfully broken by a side-panel advertising for the* Mid-Sussex Times.

Middle Right : *One of the first deliveries of the Leyland National Mk2 was made to Taff Ely as seen in their number 33 (FUH 33V). Under local government re-organisation in 1974, Taff-Ely District Council was formed from Pontypridd Urban District Council, and at the same time the Transport Dept's name was also changed to reflect the new authority's name.*

Bottom Right: *Although the National was not really the flavour of the month with Burnley & Pendle, they did use a few; one of these 50 (XRN 50V) is seen at Burnley Bus Station in July 1992.*

Bottom Left: *West Midlands Travel operated both Mk1 and Mk2 variants of the National with dual-door variants appearing in small numbers. In one of its hybrid livery phases West Midlands turned out 1042 (DOC 42V) in the scheme pictured here in September 1992.*

Above: *Yorkshire Traction always maintained a smart fleet and they also ran some of their Nationals for a long time, as seen with EDT 223V looking a young 17-years at Barnsley in 1997.*

Below: *Competition was fierce after bus deregulation, and most of this was aimed at the established operators by independents. One way of countering this was to set up a 'low cost' unit, but these often appeared in a livery that the travelling public would not associate with the major operator. One such operation was the 'Big Orange'. Of course those in the know could tell that the orange Mk2 was in fact a Northern General machine in disguise, in this case UBR 662V operating out of Gateshead bus station in August 1987. It should also be noted that, once the independents had been seen off, the 'low cost' units would often 'disappear'.*

Above: *A new-livery has been applied, but it is still a case of London Country lives! In fact it is London Country North West and SNB505 (EPD 505V) is on service in Watford. Eventually Arriva would come to operate the services in this town, but meanwhile EPD 505V was one of over 100 short B series Nationals operated by London Country.*

Below: *Still recognisable as the NBC dual-purpose livery (Leaf Green and Express White), AAE 663V is seen plying its trade around Bristol in August 1983 as it comes to the end of its 41X service. This dual-purpose livery did not appear on many Mk2 Nationals, as most of the deliveries of this type were in the standard bus configuration. However Bristol Omnibus was one company that did have such vehicles in service, although they were of the pod-less variety.*

Top Right: *Here we have an interesting comparison between the old and new liveries in the period under consideration, taking Cheltenham & District 3504 (AAE 648V) as an example. It is still wearing its Poppy Red livery with a white band, and was one of the 30+ batch of 11.3-metre Mk2s delivered to Bristol Omnibus. This example, is also interesting in that it is carrying Cheltenham & District livery but has a Swindon allocation plate and furthermore is seen in Gloucester!*

Below: *Nationals all the way at Cheltenham bus depot. From the same batch as the Mk2 seen above, AAE 650V heads a mixed row of Mk1s and Mk2s at the depot entrance in July 1993. All seven have acquired the stylish new red and white livery, albeit with different styling around the windows and below the roof.*

WHITE ROSE NATIONALISM

To keep my editor happy, because he is an ardent Yorkshireman, the following selection of images show a number of Mk2s at work in the White Rose county.

Above: *As the West Yorkshire Road Car Co. comes into this selection of photos, let us look at their Mk2 1507 (PNW 600W). It is wearing the cream-banded Poppy Red livery when seen in Leeds, but it has reverted to a traditional gold fleet name.*

Bottom Left: *Nationals and palm trees are not normally bed fellows, but this overall advert blends the two together reasonably well. Still with West Yorkshire, Mk2 SWX 534W is seen at Harrogate in August 1986, with Mk1 RYG 764R behind.*

Top Right: *Sadly, many of the Nationals bought by the Scottish Bus Group were not used to the same extent as in England or Wales. Consequently, many of those from Scottish fleets were sold when an opportunity arose. One such was Mk2 DMS 23V, which was part of the Alexander Midland fleet. By 9th May 1991, it had migrated to West Riding via Sheffield United Traction and was seen in its new owner's livery at Wakefield.*

Middle Right: *The City of York was never actually a part of the county's three Ridings, but for many years its buses were operated by York-West Yorkshire, part of the West Yorkshire Road Car Co. This operation was then sold to Yorkshire Rider, and their Mk2 1340 (SWX 537W) heads away from the city's imposing railway station in May 1992.*

Bottom Right: *This Mk2 1344 (MNW 133V) was one of several Nationals acquired from West Yorkshire Road Car Co. by the West Yorkshire PTE, which itself later went on to become Yorkshire Rider. Some of these stayed in their regular haunts but others, such as 1344, found themselves allocated to former municipal bus depots like Huddersfield. The bus is seen departing on the express service from Halifax to its new home town in September 1999.*

Bottom Left: *A May 1992 view from York city walls shows a different angle on MNW132V carrying a local version of the Yorkshire Rider fleet livery. The vehicle had originated in the West Yorkshire Road Car fleet, and had been a York-allocated vehicle. The blocky red lines at the rear of the vehicles on this page are supposed to represent the Yorkshire Rider initials YR, if you hadn't guessed.*

49

Above and Bottom Left: *The fleet of the West Yorkshire PTE was drawn mainly from municipal undertakings at formation, but it also acquired some independents. One of these W R & P Bingley of Kinsley, including their United Services bus operations (Yorkshire's last bus co-operative), which was bought out in April 1977. In due course the PTE allocated three B52F 11.6m NL116L11/1R Nationals to the fleet, and decided to paint them into a version of the independent's former livery. These were fleet numbers 1331-2 (VWU 331-2X), which were new to West Yorkshire Road Car in August 1981. This pair were followed later by 1333 (YWX 333X), which had been new to West Yorkshire Road Car in June 1982. It had latterly spent a period of time at Yorkshire Rider's Huddersfield Depot, and was seen on the previous page in its green and cream livery when leaving Halifax.*

Top Right: *Both United Services and another WYPTE-acquired independent, Baddeley Brothers of Holmfirth, worked across the border into the South Yorkshire PTE area, which itself was home to a number of veritable independent service bus operators; especially around Doncaster. Here, NRP 584V is in the service of Andrews of Sheffield, who were one of a number of independents who managed to acquire examples of former Alexander Midland Mk2s.*

Middle Right: *The South Yorkshire PTE was also a user of Leyland Nationals and here we see one of those working in the county. It has been repainted in a version of the erstwhile Doncaster Corporation livery of the 1970s, to commemorate the 80th anniversary of this particular municipal fleet that had been absorbed by the Passenger Transport Executive.*

Bottom Right: *One of the biggest operators in South Yorkshire was the NBC subsidiary Yorkshire Traction. It is this firm that is the owner of 252 (OHL 252X), which was one of over 50 Mk2s that the company operated, although this fact is hidden by the revival of the Mexborough & Swinton fleet name as seen in this 1992 view taken at Doncaster.*

Bottom Left: *The registration, LRB 200W reveals this National Mk2 to be a former Trent vehicle. Trent operated a large fleet of Mk1s, but it disposed of its few Mk2s relatively early, whilst holding on to its Mk1s, and even acquiring second-hand examples. By September 1990, Mk2 LRB 200W was part of the Yorkshire Woollen District fleet. It is about to set off from Halifax on a meandering journey to Leeds.*

NORTHERN SOUL

The Mk2 Nationals were well liked in the north, and many of them were seen hard at work twixt the rivers Tyne and Tees during the 1980s.

Top Left: *Northern General were the happy owners of a large fleet, and they were one of the last major users of the National. A few were retained in the fleet in preference to Dennis Darts, although the latter were rumoured to have been sold because they would give a better return in the second hand market. Here 4708 (FTN 708W) wears the Tyne & Wear PTE livery.*

Top Right: *This Mk2 3739 (RDC 739X ,)belonging to United, is in Stockton High Street whilst on the Middlesbrough to Durham service. A problem encountered by several NBC fleets on all vehicle types was that the fleet number transfers soon came off. The United answer was to use number plates made up from the same components as those used for the vehicle registration plates.*

Middle Left: *Not many Nationals made the move from a municipal operator to a former NBC company but we have one here in the shape of A541 PCW. It entered service with Blackpool before appearing in the Tees fleet as number 3154, and photographed in Middlesbrough in 1991.*

Bottom Left: *At first sight one of the last batch of Mk2s, (FTN 714W) looks to be with an independent! Yet, Shaws of Stanley were part of Northern General, as shown by the number 4714.*

Top Right: *Reviving liveries of the companies it had absorbed in years past, became a fairly typical NBC ploy in the era after privatisation. Here we have the application of the traditional Sunderland & District livery on this Northern Group Mk2, 4706 (FTN 706W), which is seen outside Philadelphia depot with a Tyne & Wear-liveried Mk1 in the background. Two Leyland Nationals and a double-deck Bristol VR, were painted in this style, mainly as a move to stop other operators stealing the historic liveries during the deregulation period.*

Middle Right: *Following deregulation, Hartlepool introduced a service running through to Middlesbrough. After having had a love affair with the Bristol RE, when they were withdrawn from the market a small number of Nationals were purchased by this former municipal operator. Here we see KAJ 216W, one of Hartlepool's batch of Mk2s picking up in a night-time scene on Stockton High Street.*

Bottom Right: *Also, out in the dark and pictured on a Hartlepool service at Middlesbrough Bus Station on a chilly December night in 1994 we find Tees-liveried Mk2 (A140 FDC), which was formerly part of the United fleet.*

Bottom Left: *Local identities returned to the North West region, and in particular to Cumberland Motor Service's No. 371 (HHH 371V). This was one of a number of Mk2 Nationals that this fleet operated and it is seen at Workington depot. It is of course not far from the Lillyhall factory, which after its life as a bus plant stood derelict for sometime before becoming a depot for the Cumbrian haulage firm, Eddie Stobart Ltd.*

Above: *With the privatisation sell off in mind, the north and west of Cumbria, which had once been served by three distinct operations (Cumberland Motor Services, Ribble and United Automobile), saw many routes and services being vested in a much-expanded CMS. South of this area, the post-NBC Ribble underwent an identity change of livery. The move away from the standard Poppy Red quite suited the lines of the Mk2, and it was invariably kept in good condition. Here, LFR 857X awaits its next turn of duty in Ulverston on 15th August 1990.*

Below: *The 10.3-metre Mk2s found a niche in the Ribble fleet, which operated a number of these machines. Here, 877 (LFR 877X) displays Ribble's attempt to brighten up the standard NBC red with some grey, yellow and black lining when it was caught taking the sun at Preston in August 1990.*

Above: *Although probably better known as Widnes, the former municipal fleet took up the new name of Halton. They also built up a goodly collection of both Mk1 and Mk2 Nationals. Here one of their last purchases of the type, 31 (B131 SED), is seen at Widnes in October 1992. Although, this was an independent bus operator, it became a limited company wholly owned by Halton Borough Council, which makes it one of the few remaining municipal bus companies in the UK today.*

Below: *Near neighbour Crosville was once a very well-known name, and C-Line was one of the spin-off companies formed in the break up of Crosville to provide services around Macclesfield. Amongst its fleet in September 1992, was this former Ribble Mk2 which, whilst having had the Greenway treatment, has retained its original registration of LFR 875X.*

SCOTTISH SURVIVORS

Whilst many of the Scottish Nationals quietly slipped back south over the Border in the intervening years, the model was not entirely eliminated, and examples remained hard at work for many years.

Above: *Kelvin Scottish held onto its Nationals longer than many of the operators north of the Border. This one, 1150 (YFS 307W), had been new to Scottish Omnibuses in January 1981 and was in its ninth year of service when seen in Glasgow.*

Bottom Right: *Full Stagecoach livery was used for its Fife subsidiary, as displayed by Mk2 (YSX 932W) at Dunfermline in February 1994. Delivered new to Alexander Fife in December 1980, it was one of the rarer 10.3-metre models designated NL106L11/1R by Leyland.*

CHANGING COLOURS

As we draw our story to a conclusion, it is fitting to look again at the massive change of liveries that appeared on Leyland Nationals in the latter part of the 1980s and the early '90s.

Above: *Swindon bus station is the setting for this 1994 view of Mk2 11.3-metre AAE 665V. Originally part of the Bristol Omnibus fleet, independence had come in the form of privatisation with Swindon & District, which gave a new livery for 3521.*

Bottom Left: *Swindon & District frequently sent a bus to the erstwhile Severn Valley Railway bus rally and in1993 this was LN2 3523 (BHY 997V), which is just indicating to turn into the railway station forecourt at Kidderminster.*

Above: *Despite the advent of many new liveries, many of which were designed to break the slab-sided appearance of the National, several of the older styles lasted into the second-half of the 1980s in their old colour schemes. For instance, South Wales Transport operated a small number of Mk2s and some of these were fitted with coach seats and as such they carried the traditional National Bus Company dual-purpose livery. One of these 'survivors' is seen at Swansea in October 1986, this being Mk2 818 (CCY 818V).*

Below: *In stark contrast, under Go Ahead Group-ownership, Brighton & Hove introduced some striking liveries. The use of diagonal dividing lines on a predominantly cream background gave their Mk2 National fleet an eye-catching new look, as shown off by 154 (C451 OAP) in Brighton on 30th April 1997.*

Above: *Think back to those dual-purpose Nationals delivered to Midland Red, six of which were Mk2 models. Eventually its successor, Midland Red West came into the Badgerline group and this vehicle (A204 YWP) gravitated south west to Bristol where it was pictured in action in 1989.*

Below: *Another striking livery is seen on this member of the Chesterfield fleet. Actually, No.55 (B155 DHL) represents nearly the end of the line for the National as the first Leyland Lynx was due off the production line in less than twelve months. This example was photographed on 25th April 1995, whilst working service 43 to Sheffield. However, of more interest is the roof-line banner, which states "Under New Ownership - 350 Caring Owners", which reflects the fact that this was a staff buy-out of the former Municipal undertaking.*

CAPITAL IDEAS

Finally, and though we have not covered them to any great extent, Nationals were common sights around the nation's capital, appearing in both red and green liveries. Examples from visiting fleets could also be seen on a regular basis.

Above: *At first glance, this is not a normal London express coach. However, the City of Portsmouth operated three rare coach-seated 10.6-metre Mk2s, the final one of the batch being 100 (CPO 100W), captured on film at Victoria in August 1985.*

Bottom Left: *London Transport took their final delivery of Nationals as dual door LN2s, these all being allocated to Red Arrow routes. Typical of the batch was LS458 (GUW 458W).*

Top Right: *Towards the end of their working lives in London, some of the LN2s were re-built for further use, including London Country who had some of their vehicles re-built in the Greenway programme. Hiding its true age, by carrying Northern Ireland registration plates (NIW 6507) was wearing fleet number 347, when it was seen wearing a multi-coloured livery in Isleworth in 1993.*

Below: *Those vehicles that featured in the re-building programme for the London-based Mk2 models, can be identified by the area around the front screen. Here, GUW 493W is seen hard at work on a Red Arrow service in the ownership of London General, part of the Go Ahead Group. By the time this view was taken in 1995, this batch of Nationals had been active in the capital for 20-years.*

Above: *This modified National has had the 'Greenway' treatment by East Lancashire Coach Builders in order to prolong its working life. As 2157, it carries a Northern Ireland registration plate (JIL 2157) and is working a Midland Fox 'park and ride' service in Leicester.*

Bottom Left: *The Cheltenham & Gloucester group, of which Stroud Valley was a member, rebuilt a number of the their Leyland Nationals as National IIIs. An example of this interesting conversion is seen here at Swindon Bus Station.*

Acknowledgements

This pictorial record has been a very personal journey into the history of the Leyland National, but I must thank the team at Trans-Pennine Publishing and Ian Chancellor for all their help in compiling the book!